The Art of Thought

NATHANIEL MICKLEM

The Art of Thought

LONDON

EPWORTH PRESS

Set in 12 on 13 pt Bembo

Printed by C. Nicholls & Company Ltd
London and Manchester

SBN 7162 0165 8

Contents

Acknowledgements

The author and publisher acknowledge, with thanks, permission to quote from the publications of George Allen and Unwin, Collins, Oxford University Press.

Preface

MANY YEARS AGO Stephen Paget adumbrated a book to be entitled *The Boys' Own Berkeley*; it was to take the leading ideas of the philosopher-bishop and set them forth in language to be readily grasped by the schoolboy of intelligence. It is something along these lines that I have attempted in this book.

I am not addressing myself to professional philosophers and academics, though I would profit by their comments. I am writing for thoughtful people today who having no philosophical training yet wish to look beneath the surface of things, and who are deeply perplexed and troubled when they ponder such profound and fundamental questions as whether anything is worth while, whether in the end life has any meaning beyond such pleasure as we may be able to snatch from it, whether Nature as the biologists, the chemists and the mathematical physicists reveal it to us serves any purpose, whether our mental life, our ideals, our longings, our eager purposes are not as evanescent and ultimately insignificant as a morning mist, whether in fact *things* are and *we* only seem to be. If under the influence of 'scientific thought' we must abandon religion which once gave meaning and significance to human life, is there anything, any philosophy, any right way of thinking that will replace it for us?

Such matters are profoundly discussed in many learned books, but the readers I have in mind are too busy and perhaps not sufficiently interested to read such books. One cannot make difficult questions easy without distortion, but at least I have tried to write simply and not superficially about great issues which are usually confined to learned works, and which yet, as I believe, not only concern every thoughtful man but can also be made intelligible to him. I shall be forgiven, I hope, if in the interests of clarity I am guilty of some repetition which in a technical treatise would be reprehensible. I shall be very content if any ordinary thoughtful reader will say of my book that I have widened his horizons, stimulated his imagination and quickened in him awe or wonder.

Now, if we are to think of these great questions of human destiny, of the meaning of life, of Nature and of human society, where are we to start? There is today a considerable number of influential teachers, some of them (very curiously) holding chairs of philosophy in our Universities, who tell us not to start at all! The world, they tell us, is what it is, and all the philosophical questions we raise and discuss about it are simply word-games that we care to play. Their assurance that the world is what it is brings no great mental illumination to us, for

8

we knew that already. But these teachers subtly insinuate that this world is what it seems to be (and what it ought to be), and these are much more questionable propositions.

Whereas in old days men turned to the Bible to find an answer to their questionings, we are now instucted by these new-style philosophers that, because the world is what it is, we must be content to refer to the dictionary to tell us what words mean and what things are. Of such teachers we may say with Viola, 'they that dally nicely with words may quickly make them wanton'.[1]

This method of solving or repudiating our troublesome questioning saves us the bother of trying to think things out for ourselves, but the thoughtful man is insatiably curious, and there are moments of special puzzlement or illumination in the lives of all of us, when we are oppressed with a sense of the mystery that surrounds our lives and are made aware of longings or of visions or, as Wordsworth called them, 'intimations' that transcend our day to day experience. We know such moments. What are we to make of them?

There is abroad a very widespread and widely assumed principle that nothing is to be believed that cannot be proved scientifically or by irrefutable logic. Many, especially those whose training is exclusively scientific, profess this principle, but no one, as I suppose, actually lives by it. It is, if I may venture to say so, intrinsically silly. A man

[1] In this connection a very widely influential book has been A. J. Ayer's, *Language, Truth and Logic*, Gollancz, 1946. Cf. E. Gellner, *Words and Things*, Penguin.

knows very well that he loves his wife and children and is certain of their love for him, but no logic can prove these convictions nor scientific method verify them. This view is not only silly, it is self-contradictory. We are asked to accept the proposition, 'nothing is to be accepted as true that is not open to logical or scientific proof', but this principle itself is not open to logical or scientific proof; it is pure assumption and on its own showing is not to be accepted as a truth. I shall not waste time on this current absurdity but beg any reader who has been brought up to think along these lines to consider on what sands he builds.

In my first three chapters I have dealt with fundamental questions usually called 'philosophical' or 'speculative' and handed over as such to specialists in whose hands they become 'as dry as a remainder biscuit after a voyage' and as abstract as a problem in the higher mathematics. Yet these issues are of great practical significance, for our daily life is profoundly influenced by what we think in our hearts or 'at the back of our minds' about ourselves and about the world of things and of living Nature round about us. I shall be disappointed if I have not managed to make these questions interesting and intelligible to the inquisitive and thoughtful reader.

In my next chapter I am concerned with man as a being who is touched by a sense of beauty, moved to seek for truth, conscious of obligations and aware of what I may best describe as a mysterious Beyond. In my epilogue I indicate my own conclusions and presume to offer a suggestion to the hesitant and puzzled reader.

The original instigation to the writing of this short essay came to me from reading (in the English translation) a vast treatise in two huge volumes entitled *Microcosmus* by the philosopher Hermann Lotze. The author was well abreast of the scientific thought of his day, but now he is out of date. I cannot think that the ordinary reader will attempt an old book which even most philosophers today have, as I fear, neglected, but my debt must be acknowledged. When I was a young man sixty years ago, I was told that none of the philosophers ever mentions Lotze because they all owe their souls to him. That, of course, was in days when philosophers were more sure that they had souls than are many now.

Two other books have influenced me much as I have been writing the pages following. One is Sir Alister Hardy's Gifford Lectures, *The Divine Flame*, in which he stresses the intimate connection between man and the rest of the animal kingdom from which he is emerging; the other is Sir Malcolm Knox' Gifford Lectures, *Action*, in which, contrariwise, he stresses the essential difference between man and the natural order which he transcends. Other debts are too many and too various for mention here, except only that I must thank my philosopher son, Robert Deverell Micklem, of Bradford, for his admonitions, corrections and advice.

'Every book', wrote J. L. Synge, 'is a protest against the loneliness that wraps around each of us'. We must think alone, as we must die alone, and it is only in some degree that we can share our thoughts. 'Strange is our situation here upon earth', said Albert Einstein; 'each of us comes for a short visit, not knowing why, yet sometimes seeming to divine a purpose'. In the pages that follow I have sought to share my thoughts with any who may care to read them. I have appealed to his insight and hoped for his consent. We are apt to regard thinking as the operation of the mind alone, and this may be nearly true of thinking in the fields of science and mathematics, but mind is an abstraction from the whole of our personality, and even in those restricted fields there can be no thinking without some element of willing and of feeling. More particularly when we are considering the great ultimate questions of life and destiny it is required of us that we think with all our faculties and our whole personality. My little book might be termed a tentative introduction to what Carlyle calls 'the grand thaumaturgic art of Thought'.

I

Man as an Individual

IT IS WELL known that the philosopher, Descartes, seeking for an unshakeable basis for his philosophy, determined to start by doubting everything that can be doubted. By this method he arrived at the simple proposition, 'I think, therefore I am'. His own existence, he found, he could not doubt. The difficulty about this starting-point is that from our own existence as thinkers we cannot legitimately or logically jump to the existence of anything else. Might Descartes not as well have said, 'I dream, therefore I am'? In Gertrud Von Le Fort's novel, *The Veil of Veronica*, Descartes' saying was being discussed at table. The servant girl interrupted the conversation; 'that's nothing', she said, 'I pray, therefore I am'. That is better; but few people would accept the argument that because I pray to God, therefore God is to whom I pray.

I

It might be thought that no man could possibly deny his own existence, yet, most curiously, that is precisely what a vast number of people in the modern world implicitly deny. The argument runs like this: all our impressions of the outside world come to us through our brains; every idea in our heads, every effort of will that we make, every ideal that we espouse has its counterpart in the brain; apart from our brain, therefore, there can be no feeling, thinking or willing; all our conscious mental life arises from modifications of our brain; when, therefore, our brain wholly ceases to function, we cease to be. This is not to deny that in some sense we exist. An orange is a yellow object; the yellowness exists, but it exists in the orange; apart from the orange it has no separate existence of its own. The orange, as we say grammatically, is a substantive, the yellowness an adjective. It is with our brains that we think; the brain in a living person is a thinking object; there is no 'I' or self that exists apart from the brain; the brain, therefore, is the substantive; thinking, feeling and willing are adjectival. In earlier days it was supposed that man consists of body and soul, the two being here most intimately connected, no doubt, but separate realities such that the soul would not be destroyed with the destruction of the body. A very common view today is that we have no souls possessing an independent existence of this kind.

The old term 'soul' I shall generally avoid, for it

has religious connotations, nor in this chapter shall I treat of character or personality. I am here solely concerned with the view that our mental life is an exhalation from our brains like the scent emitted from a flower; remove the flower and the scent is dissipated. I propose to offer reasons for supposing that our mental life is not merely adjectival, that we exist, and that our real existence is not a mere illusion thrown off by our active brains.

Behaviourism is the professional or technical name for the view that all our mental life and all our conduct are but reflex action or passion of movements within our brain, that we are in fact automata; we think that we form our own judgements by cogitation and make our choices by voluntary decision, but in fact we are only reflecting in the form of thought the movements of our brains and of our bodily organism.

There is some evidence to support this view. 'When the endocrine glands sicken, the mind sickens also'; if a friend is suffering from depression, the best advice to him may be to take a pill; our thoughts and judgements are apt to be qualified by the state of our bodies or the outward circumstances in which we find ourselves; an operation on the brain may have, at least apparently, the most untoward effects upon our character. On the other hand, as all physicians know, the health of our bodies is closely related to the state of our minds; indeed, we do not know the limits of the influence of mind on body. Furthermore, our bodies can be wasted, while our minds remain alert and firm;

our mind can be clear when our body is at the point of death. There is clearly a reciprocal relation between body and mind, but we look at only one side of the evidence if we maintain that our mental life is a mere reflection of our bodily states.

Again, the view that all our sensations, all our emotions, all our thoughts and our actions are caused by stimulations of our brains cannot without contradiction be defended as *true*, for truth, which is relative to mind, in that case will have lost its meaning; one man's opinions differ from another's as the scent of a rose differs from the scent of garlic, but one scent is not more true than another; both are actual. If opinions are determined by our bodily organs, then all opinions are equally actual, and none is more true than another. The theory that we are really automata, that our mental life is but the offspring of processes of the brain, is put before us as an explanation of our mental life, but, as Sir Malcolm Knox puts it, 'a theory claims to be *true;* its sponsors ask us to *choose* it and to reject as false a theory that contradicts it. Determinism is a theory which denies the possibility of choice and it therefore refutes itself'.[1] If we are automata, it is silly to ask us to make a choice, or to suggest that one choice is more true than another.

In another field there are psychologists who have learnt much from the pioneer work of Freud and would persuade us that the things we do, whatever we suppose our motive to be, and our attitudes to people, however rational we reckon them, are in

[1] *Action*, Allen and Unwin, 1968, p. 73; italics mine—N.M.

fact the result, not of the motions of our brains, but of the workings and complexes of our unconscious minds. We have much to learn from these teachers about ourselves and about other people. Our attitude and responses to persons and events may be much more automatic, because inspired by hidden complexes, than we suspect, but it is the task and calling of these psychologists to deliver us from our bonds, and it is agreed that when our hidden complexes are brought to consciousness, we can deal with them and be liberated from them. Intimate, then, as is the connection between mind and body, the mind can triumph over the infirmities of the body and be liberated from the bonds of the unconscious. In our mental life we are, or at least we can be, more than a mere reflection of our bodily states or our unconscious.

Physiologists or psychologists or philosophers in their studies may accept the theory of Behaviourism, that we are in fact automata and that our mental life is determined by causes hidden from our consciousness, but no man lives as if he believed this theory. If a man comes into my study while I am working and says, 'Look it is a lovely day; chuck what you are doing and have a round of golf with me!', I must think quickly. I should much prefer a round of golf to managing my typewriter, and a round would doubtless do me good; but how am I ever to get through my work, which I know I ought to do, if I let myself be diverted in this way, and how shall I not lose my train of thought? One of these electro-encephalographic machines would doubtlessly record all the movements of my brain as I painfully come to my decisions; the brain may record *my* thoughts and *my* emotional struggles, but to suppose that the cerebral mass inside my skull does the thinking and deciding, while I, who think I am deciding, am a mere automatom seems very great nonsense. If I really *believed* that I am a mere automaton, I should not wrestle with my conscience; I should merely wait to see what happened! But, even so, *I* should wait to see; there is no getting away from '*I*'.

II

Every operation of the mind may, perhaps, be recorded in the brain, but the mind is not to be regarded as a mere function of the brain. If I cannot remember a name or word that eludes me, I 'cudgel my brains' to find it. If I would write an essay I must use my brains; it is not really sense in this case to think of my brains using me and creating the mind, the 'me', that they are using. If I say, 'I believe I am only an illusion, the creation of my brain', I have contradicted myself in saying this, for I have expressed a belief, a theory, and no theory can escape from the '*I*' that maintains it; the brain is always something that 'I' know. I am intuitively aware of my own existence, but being no scientist I should never have known that my brain exists unless somebody had told me, or I had read it in a book.

The mind *interprets* that which through the nervous system is presented to it by the brain.

Here I may use an illustration I have employed elsewhere: I may see an object made of gold: I may read the word gold in print; I may feel the idea of gold through my finger if I can read braille; I may hear the spoken word in a deep bass voice or hear it on the high note of a child. In each of these cases the brain has received through the nervous system a quite distinct impression different from all the others, but in all these cases the *mind* at once apprehends the single idea of 'gold'. It gives one interpretation to many different signs. Or, again, the colours of the rainbow may be painted vertically on a cylinder; let this cylinder be revolved at a very high speed before my eyes; the brain is receiving a series of quite different impressions, one colour after another, but what my *mind* receives and what I see is one mixed colour.

The mind, in fact, interprets the data of the senses as they are transmitted through the brain. The light-waves and sound-waves which are passed on to the brain through electrical discharges and are received by us in the form of colours and of sound are not themselves either colourful or resonant; there is neither light nor sound in the brain itself. Again, I feel something to be hard or soft or hot or cold, but hardness and softness, heat and cold are in the mind, not in the brain. When a chord is played upon the piano, the different sounds which the brain transmits are received as a unity by the mind.[1] In all these cases it is the mind that interprets the

[1] *And I know not if, save in this, such gift be allowed to man,*
That out of three sounds he frame, not a fourth sound, but a star.
—Robert Browning in *Abt Vogler*.

data presented to it, most mysteriously and in-explicably, through the senses by the brain.

All our human experience is, we suppose, re-corded on our brain, but in respect of the mind the brain, if I may use quite untechnical terms, plays sometimes an active and sometimes a passive part. I am calling the brain active when it stimulates the mind by the presentation of sense impressions. I am calling it passive when it receives instructions from the mind. When I have decided what response to make to the invitation to play golf, I shall either stretch out my arm to pick up my golf-clubs, or I shall raise my hands to get on with my typing. Neither of these muscular activities can be achieved except through the brain, but the brain is here my obedient servant. Bodily stimulations exist for consciousness after they have been transmitted *from* the brain; mental stimulations exist for the body only after being conveyed *to* the brain.

This distinction is so important for our thinking that I venture yet another illustration: by some stimulus of the brain I am conscious, let us say, of a map on the page before me, or, rather, I am con-scious of impressions which I interpret as a map. I distinguish colours on it; I note mathematical relations such as the lines of longitude or latitude; I judge distances to be great or small; I note that some sections are larger than others; I make up my mind whether the map is likely to be of use to me on the journey which I plan. Here, when I receive the im-pression or series of impressions (which I later interpret as a map), the brain, as concerns my mind, plays an active role. But when I make judgements about the map, distinguish colours on it (there are no colours in the brain), estimate mileage and distance and decide that the map will, or will not, be useful to me, these judgements are recorded on the brain, but the brain here plays a passive part; it is the recipient of my thoughts. The thinking and the judging is done by *me* and is recorded on my brain. It is *I* who do the thinking, not the brain.

III

We think by means of concepts. A concept in this connection is a term applicable to many different examples. If I see a book on my table, I have received a visual stimulus from my brain. It may be oddly bound, and at first I may not recognize it for what it is; but, once I have identified it as a book, I have brought my sensation under a concept which covers unnumbered other objects. If I should say, 'the book I am now writing is intended to make difficult philosophical notions more easily intelligible', I should have brought together many concepts, book, attempt, notions, intelligibles. Since I am a human being, I could not say this without using my brain, but it is *I* who use my brain, not a brain that uses a 'me' which is but a function or emanation of itself.

Euclid's demonstration of his theorems in old school-books ends always with the letters Q.E.D. (*quod erat demonstrandum*). If you had followed his argument, you were compelled by a necessity of your mind to agree, for instance, that the angles at the base of an isosceles triangle are equal, and that if the equal sides be produced, the exterior angles will be also equal. It is surely the very queerest and most improbable assumption that the brain has substantial reality but that the mind which apprehends the truth is merely adjectival to the brain.

Besides, the idea that physical things are real and things of the mind unreal, mere epiphenomena, as they are called, leads to ridiculous conclusions. For instance, I see certain black marks printed on a piece of paper; these are the physical sensible reality presented to me by my brain. I read these marks as setting out a problem in algebra. Is the problem less real than the printed signs? Is it merely, as someone put it, 'a ghost inhabiting an ink-patch'? No one *believes* that!

Many who do not accept the view that consciousness is a mere illusion thrown off by the brain are yet apt to speak of an intimate interaction of mind and body. But strictly this is not a correct expression. If two objects are to interact, they must be external to one another; but the mind is not an object in space outside the body, nor can the mind be described as an object inside the brain, for the mind cannot be located in space; it is not an object; it is a subject. Psychologists can study very fruitfully the way in which men's minds have seemed to work; but if they can study the manifest operations (or even the hidden operations) of mind, they cannot directly study mind itself. They can study 'the psychical faculties', but the mind is a subject, not an object.

IV

The mind is a subject. It is true that I can study myself, my thoughts and intentions, my hopes and fears as an object of my thought, but it is still I as subject that consider myself as object. The 'I' is, to use technical terms, a transcendental unity of apperception. It is, as Lotze puts it, 'the substantial and permanent subject of the phenomena of our inner life'.[1] Of this 'I' we are intuitively conscious. Self-consciousness rests upon a direct and immediate sense of self; we do not derive it from contemplating that which is not ourselves; it is presupposed and experienced in that contemplation. It is the subject of all thought and all experience. Lotze puts it in this way: 'our belief in the soul's unity rests not on our appearing to ourselves such a unity, but upon our being able to appear to ourselves *at all*. . . . What a being appears to itself to be is not the important point; if it can appear anyhow to itself, or other things to it, it must be capable of unifying manifold phenomena in an absolute indivisibility of its nature'.[2] The mind or self is the identity of the perceiving subject.

I must at this point raise a question to which, at least at the present stage of my argument, no satisfactory answer can be given. I have offered reasons for supposing that the mind or the self or, as it used to be called, the soul exists and is not to be identified with the brain and physical constitution with which it is so closely allied. If the mind or self

[1] *Op. cit.*, I. 389.   [2] *Op. cit.*, I. 157.

of which we are conscious depends for its operation upon our brains, then it would seem to follow that when our brains cease to function, we cease to be, as many now suppose. In that case our human life has no ultimate significance; meaningful as it seems to be while we are living it, in the end it comes to nothing. Perhaps it would not necessarily follow that the whole universe itself is meaningless. Meaning exists only for mind, but we might, I suppose, imagine some infinite Mind for which existence would be meaningful, but that would be cold comfort. The Hebrew people for centuries had an overwhelming sense of God without draw- ing any corollary of personal immortality. At present I only raise the question whether it is con- ceivable that the self, the mind, should continue after the body's death.

The physicians are finding it very difficult or even impossible to define the exact moment when death occurs, but in any case the death of the mind or the self, if it occurs, is not to be identified with the moment of physical death. Many a patient lies in a coma for days before he dies, and it would be difficult to maintain that the mind or self is still there in the failing body. In such cases we should have to say that the mind, the self, if it dies, dies some while before the body.

I am not satisfied that the psychical researchers have *proved* the continued existence of persons after the death of the body, but the evidence they have amassed is certainly impressive, and we should reckon with the possibility or even probability that before long they will have proved to the scientific mind that the death of the body does not carry with it the non-existence of the self. Such a demonstration of continuity would not prove anything like immortality, but it would fortify my argument that the self or mind is not to be identified with the physical body.

Man has not had any difficulty in *imagining* disembodied spirits, and there is no philosophic difficulty in supposing that the self, which under the conditions of mortality, has been aware of its surroundings and has expressed its purposes through a brain and a physical body, might under other conditions be aware of its surroundings and express its purposes through some other kind of body (if that be the right term) appropriate to new conditions. I see no difficulty in supposing that this *might be* so; whether or not we should believe that it *is* so depends upon considerations to which we have not yet come.

V

We are apt to distinguish between being and knowing on the understanding that the universe consists of being, and that knowing is a more or less accurate cognitive reflection of what is. Certainly many things exist that we do not know, and all our knowledge is partial and imperfect. But if anything were intrinsically unknowable, that is, not merely beyond the knowledge of human beings but unknowable by Mind or an infinite Mind, it could not be said to exist at all. To exist is to exist for mind; knowability is what we mean by existence. It is anomalous to suggest that knowing is the result of something else existing (the brain) since the existence of the brain already presupposes mind. To put the matter more simply, it was a long time before man discovered that he had a brain, but had the brain been unknowable, not there to be discovered and known, there would be no sense in speaking of the existence of the brain. Not in time but in logic knowing is prior to being, for apart from knowing being has no meaning. The mind of man, though it arises in nature, is distinct from nature.

This idea is strange till we are familiar with it. Let me, therefore, put it another way: there is a real world of our sensible experience; if it were not a real world, we could not make mistakes about it. We cannot make mistakes about what happens in our dreams, but we can, and often do, make mistakes about the world of things. But we cannot have any knowledge of things as they are apart from mind, for mind is required for the understanding of nature, and in the next chapter we shall see how large is the contribution of mind to all our observations. Scientists investigate the 'laws of nature' or the natural order, but 'laws' and 'order' exist for mind; they are not things.

Here is another element in mind, the significance of which will appear more clearly in the sequel: no finite achievement can ever satisfy the mind; the more we know, the more we want to know, and the more we are conscious of our ignorance, for potentially or in principle mind is infinite[1].

[1] *v.* Knox, *op. cit.*, p. 49.

VI

I must take one further step. If I say that I am I, I am implicitly meaning that I am not you nor anybody else. We are only aware of ourselves in relation to, and in distinction from, other human beings. Each of us is a private and largely incommunicable centre of consciousness, but this is a consciousness of that which is not ourselves. There could be no consciousness which is a consciousness of nothing, for that would be unconsciousness. Our self-consciousness is a consciousness of people and of things.

Further, it is only in relation to other people that we are aware of the reality of things. If at a party I should go to the window and say, 'a coach and four has just driven up to the front door', and if everyone present rushing to the window assured me that there was no coach and four, and if I still claimed to see it, I should be well advised to consult a doctor. When we call a thing real, we mean that it is part of a world common to us all; our experience of the real world without us is, or is in principle, a shared experience. If my eyesight is better than my companions', I may say that I see a ship at sea which they cannot see but 'get a telescope', I shall say, and *then* if they do not see the ship, I shall know I was mistaken. A scientist makes his solitary experiment, but says to all other scientists, 'if you will repeat my experiment, you will find what I have found'. Not till his result has been verified by a common or shared experience will it be accepted as an element in the real world. It is only in a world of other persons that we are aware or assured of the reality of things.

In this chapter, then, I have offered reasons for supposing that our mind, our self, our mental life has its own existence in distinction from the body with which it is so closely associated, that it is no mere emanation of the brain, adjectival to it, that each of us is an ultimate unity of apperception such that even if I say, 'I do not exist', I have claimed existence by saying 'I'. Further, I have argued that the self or 'I' has no existence in lone aseity, as the philosophers call it; it exists only in relation to that which is not I. More, my assurance of the reality of things depends upon a logically prior relation to other persons. Instead, therefore, of Descartes' starting point, 'I think, therefore I am', we had better say, 'I am intuitively aware of myself in a world of persons and of things'.

With one more quotation from Lotze, I will end this chapter. He writes:

Materialism may prolong its existence and celebrate its triumphs within the schools, where so many ideas estranged from life find shelter, but its own professors will deny their false creed in their living action. For they will continue to love and hate, to hope and fear, to dream and study, and they will in vain seek to persuade us that this varied existence of mental energies, which even deliberate denial of the super-sensible cannot destroy, is a product of their bodily organization, or that the love of truth exhibited by some, the sensitive vanity betrayed by others, has its origin in their cerebral fibres. Among all the errors of the human mind it has always seemed to me the strangest that it could come to doubt its own existence, of which alone it has direct experience, or to take it at second hand as the product of an external Nature which we know only indirectly, only by means of the knowledge of the very mind to which we would fain deny existence.[1]

[1] *Op. cit.*, I. 263.

2

Things

WHAT IS a thing? To many the question will sound foolish. Do we not know quite well what things are, for are we not dealing with them every day? We may raise difficult questions about the existence of minds or souls, but when we are dealing with things, we have before us sensible entities the reality of which we cannot doubt. It may give us pause, however, to reflect that of mind we have immediate consciousness, but of things we have only a knowledge mediated through the senses. Up to a point we know what mind is; we do not know what things really are. The familiarity of daily use and the excitement of scientific discovery hide from us the mystery that surrounds the commonest objects of our daily life.

What do we mean by 'a thing'? Change goes on all the time; even the granite mountains are gradually and imperceptibly undergoing change; no man can ever step in the same river twice. No physical object remains absolutely the same from age to age or even from day to day. I shall define a thing as an object of sense which, so long as it lasts, remains identifiable in spite of all the changes that take place within it and around it.

I

I alluded earlier to the view, now very commonly accepted, that nothing is to be believed that cannot be measured or verified by scientific experiment. But on this principle we are not justified in believing in the existence of things at all! 'Belief in the existence of material objects cannot be established by any appeal to verifiability.'[1] We wish to prove that things exist in their own right apart from our experience of them, but how could we measure or verify by scientific experiment anything apart from our consciousness of it? The existence of things cannot be verified apart from our experience of them. I am prepared to leave that rather difficult metaphysical argument being content to say that we know that things exist because we are aware of them. We can make mistakes about them, but we could not make mistakes about the world, if there were not a real world for us to live in.

Up to a point students of the evolutionary process

[1] Peter R. Baelz, *Christian Theology and Metaphysics*, Epworth, 1968, p. 111.

can tell us how things came to be what they are. They explain how the great mountains were thrown up, how the valleys were gradually formed by water pressure, how the wild horse gradually developed into the beautiful creature that wins the Derby; if we visit a factory we can see how machine-made goods come to be. But how the Whole, the universe, came to be eludes our imagination altogether. Here the wonder is not that any particular thing should be but that anything should be at all. We can imagine, or think that we can imagine, nothingness, but even so it is we who are imagining it. The name we usually give to this unimaginable mystery is 'Creation', a name for a wholly baffling mystery. It is, I think, equally impossible for us to imagine the total end of the physical universe, the whole disappearing without remainder, leaving not a wrack behind. We must accept the fact that we are and that things are, but, once again, what are things?

II

In the first place things are real or actual but are not what they seem.[1]

As a background it is well to bear in mind what the physicists now tell us. For long years it was supposed that all material objects are constructed of

[1] I prefer 'actual' to 'real', because I want to keep the word 'real' for ultimate Reality, but, as the word is normally used, I want to insist that the world of our sensible experience is a real, not an imaginary, world, though it is not what it seems.

tiny, solid particles called atoms. An atom is by definition that which cannot be divided. In recent years we have split the atom discovering the enormous power that lies within it. The physicists now tell us of protons and electrons and molecules and various sub-atomic particles. If we press them still further, they will tell us, I gather, that we must postulate ultimate units of energy, but this is a little further than the imagination of man will reach, for sometimes they find it convenient or necessary to speak of these units as particles and sometimes as vibrations or as waves; but strictly a unit of energy cannot be a particle, which, however infinitesimal, is an extended and material thing as energy is not, and again there cannot be vibrations if there is nothing there to be vibrated. We stop here, not because we question the findings of the physicists, but because thought itself is baffled. It is well to bear in mind this ultimate mystery of matter, but I will not dwell upon it because the world of our experience, that is, the world as known to us through our senses is not the world as described by the atomic physicists.

I come, then, to sensation and the wonder that underlies it. By 'things' we normally mean objects as we feel or taste or smell or see or hear them. But what is the relation between what we feel and that which gives rise to our feelings? What is the connection, for instance, between the light whereby we see and the vibrations which, according to the scientists, cause us to be aware of light? Light shines, but it shines for sight alone; it can have no meaning for a man born blind. When in the garden we look at the flowers and hear the wind in the trees and the song of birds, this experience is caused in us, we are told, by light-waves and sound-waves striking upon the retina of the eye and the ear's drum. From eye and ear there is an electrical discharge to the brain, and we see colours and hear sounds. But light-waves are not coloured, and sound-waves are not noisy; they are vibrations. Similarly the electrical discharges to the brain are neither colourful nor resounding, nor, again, is colour or sound within the brain itself. By some mysterious alchemy, which there is no explaining, the mind, stimulated by the brain, sees colours and hears sounds.

If we are to speak strictly or scientifically, we should not say that the grass is green, for from the scientific point of view each blade of grass is a relatively stable mass of molecules or electrons or units of energy which have no colour. When we say that the grass is green, we are meaning (unless it be in time of drought) that any normal human being seeing grass in daylight will have the sensation of greenness or viridity. The same principle applies to all sensations. I can truthfully say that the table on which I write is a continuum both firm and solid. That is a fact of human experience, but it is not a scientific fact, as the physicists make plain to us. Sugar is sweet, but sweetness has no meaning except in relation to the sense of taste; the sweetness is in the mind and experience of the percipient, not in the thing itself. The world of things that we know is the world of our common human experience; it is relative to our human senses; it is a real or actual world, though it is a world quite different from that contemplated by atomic physicists. The world of our experience is the world as it seems to man with his five physical senses. Things are phenomena, that is, appearances. Of what ultimately they are appearances even the wisest men of science cannot tell us.

III

It might seem a glaring and irresponsible paradox if I were to say this solid tangible world of things is created by mind and apart from mind has no existence, but it would not be far from truth. Red and yellow, light and dark, above and below, thick and thin, hard and soft are elements in our experience. We agree that things are red or yellow, light or dark, above or below, thick or thin, hard or soft because all have the same or very similar sensations in respect of these objects. These qualities belong to the common world of sensible human experience. So we say that notes are sharp or flat, loud or soft. These differences or experiences exist for the mind alone; they are facts or truths of human experience; they are not scientific truths about electrons.

It may be objected that even here we are dealing with scientific facts because we can measure the vibrations of light-waves and sound-waves, and know that light-waves of a certain range of vibrations will be apprehended by man as red or yellow; but we cannot know, and have no satisfactory reason for supposing, that these same vibrations striking upon the eye of a hawk or butterfly cause them to see red and yellow. A geranium is really red, and a cowslip is really yellow; by 'really' we mean here that it is so in the world of human experience, in the world of things as man apprehends them. But since the sensible qualities of things are simply the impressions which the human mind receives, we come very near to saying that the mind itself creates the world of our experience. But we must not quite say that. There is a real or actual world, not merely a seeming world, of our experience. It is a world that our curiosity can more and more discover. There are the light-waves, the sound-waves, the electrons and molecules and atoms, the electrical discharges which through the instrumentality of the brain are the causes of our sensations. Things are more than bundles of sensations as Berkeley thought; in some way they are really there.

IV

All sciences, we say, tend to become more and more mathematical. In particular only a mathematician can understand modern physics and astrophysics. We count the vibrations of the note given out by a violin; the snowflakes form themselves or are formed into regular geometrical patterns; the world below and beyond the level of our immediate sensations is a mathematical world. In olden days men spoke of 'the music of the spheres'; this we now regard as mythology, but music with the laws of harmony is capable of mathematical representation. Indeed, Lotze could speak of mathematics as 'desiccated music'.[1] But mathematics is an abstract intellectual discipline concerned not with things but with enumeration. It is an operation of the mind.[2] The scientists do not *impose* upon the universe the innumerable mathematical patterns of molecules, electrons, crystals, snowflakes; they *find* them there. What we call the laws of nature are mathematical or can only be expressed satisfactorily in mathematical form. Since mathematics is a discipline of the intellect, we are bound to say that the intellect of man finds the operation of Intellect in nature. In so far as science is mathematical it may be described as mind discovering Mind. This is obvious and would, I think, be at once accepted by all men except for their fear that once they have admitted Mind spelled with a capital letter, they will be further committed to all sorts of theological propositions which are not involved in this admission. Let me make it plain, therefore, that Mind here is correlative only to mathematics. It is not really open to us to maintain that the mathematical regularities of nature are the result of chance. Science in so far as it is mathematical is mind exploring Mind.

---

[1] *Op. cit.*, II. 442.

[2] 'Is not Mathematics indeed the most obvious pattern and standard of what we mean by Pure Reason?' R. S. Franks *The Atonement*, Oxford, p. 110.

All our experience of the objective world of things is spatial. Things 'occupy space', as we loosely say; but space is not a thing like a bag which can be filled with other things; if it were, the scientists could isolate it, experiment with it and study it. All material objects are spatially related to one another, and space is real in the sense that about spatial relations we can make mistakes. When I open my eyes, I receive a visual impression; at once my mind begins to sort this out; one thing, I say, is near at hand, another at a distance; one thing is above or behind another. This is really a matter of mathematics, a measurement of relative distances. This distinction of distances since our infancy we make quite unconsciously, but spatial relations are not given in the sensible impressions themselves; they are a contribution or interpretation of the mind. Space is not a thing but a form of human experience; it is by a necessity of our minds that all our experience of the external world is spatially related.

Time seems more real, for things really change, and they can only change in time. But time is never given us in the impressions made upon our senses. We have no physical organ of time as we have of sight and sound. A cow in the fields may hear from a distance a peal of bells. It is the mind of man which apprehends the notes as a succession of related notes and as a tune. Simultaneity and succession are mental concepts or judgements of the mind. Time like place is not a thing to be isolated and studied by the scientists; it is a relation between events, an interpretation made by mind.

These last two paragraphs must, I am afraid, inevitably be difficult at first, but the point I am making can be simply and intelligibly stated. All human experience of 'things', with which we are concerned in this chapter, is under the forms of time and space. We are so made that by a necessity of our nature our experience of the world without us is spatially and temporarily related. But sense-impressions themselves are just impressions; it is the mind that apprehends them in their spatial and temporal relations, just as it is the mind which interprets some light-waves in terms of red and others of yellow. A quality or a relation always denotes that which by its nature only has reality as a state of feeling or a judgement of some sensitive being. It is certain that our sensations are not *like* that which gives them cause, and if time and space are mental intuitions or contributions of the mind to our experience, then 'that which exists must itself be subject to an order neither spatial nor temporal, which acting upon us is by us translated into the form of spatial and temporal order'.[1]

Once more, all science, all technology and indeed all our planning and thinking about the world of experience rests upon the idea of causation. What we call 'the laws of nature' are rules of causation, as when we say that gravitation causes a heavy weight to fall to the ground. But so far as science is concerned 'cause' points to an invariable

[1] Lotze, *op. cit.* II. 349.

or very nearly invariable observable succession. We know that to touch a red-hot poker causes pain, but why or how a mental event, pain, should be caused by a physical event, touching the poker, is, if we come to think of it, utterly mysterious. How 'things' affect consciousness we cannot know. So a blush of shame amounts upon the cheek of modesty; but *how* the mind affects the body we cannot tell. Now, science can never isolate a cause and study it; it merely observes that A is invariably followed by B, and therefore says that A causes B; but the notion of cause is not given in the event itself, which is merely an invariable succession. Cause is a mental notion or intuition. All our experience of the world without us is in terms of time and space and cause, but we never directly experience any of these.

'Things' are much more mysterious than we recognize at first. Our sensible experience is an interpretation of the brain's stimuli in terms of significance for *human* life, and time, space and cause are contributions of the mind to that which we experience. How far we are from the puerile notion that, things being what they are, we shall learn what they are by reference to the dictionary and encyclopedia! With one more citation from Lotze I close this section:

All the matter of our thoughts comes to us directly or indirectly from experience; but that is not the case with the rules by which, connecting, comparing, judging and inferring, we unite and divide the matter, and pass from one thought to another. The source of these rules is not to be sought without us; the feeling of necessary and inevitable validity, with which they impose themselves on our consciousness, is, on the contrary, a guarantee that they have their origin in that from which we can never separate ourselves, namely, in the peculiar nature of our mental being. Provided with these modes of apprehension, we face the manifold throng of impressions occasioned in us by the outer world; not till we apply them does the actual sum of internal states become to us knowledge. Thus we supply as innate the intuitive forms of Space and Time to those impressions, whose mutual relations are henceforth transformed for us into the succession and contiguity of the phenomenal world of sense; thus we pass on to the observation of our data with the inevitable assumption, that all reality must rest on the foundation of enduring substances to which the variable attributes are attached as dependent and accessory; further, with the certainty that every event is bound by a causal connection as an effect to its antecedents. It is the application of these inborn beliefs that transforms our apprehension of objects into the knowledge of a universal whole made such by internal organization.[1]

VI

It is an unnecessary and self-frustrating notion that our only knowledge of things is that which we can derive from the dictionary and the text-book. I will

[1] *Op. cit.*, I. 226 f.

take water as a simple instance. Water is a liquid, or we might say it is the liquid form of that which is sometimes solid as ice, or gaseous as steam, according to differences of temperature, but what is it in itself apart from temperature? That is a foolish question; for it is meaningless to speak of water or ice or gas existing outside or apart from the universe of things; these things cannot be apart from some temperature or other. The scientific definition of water, as every schoolboy knows, is H_2O, a fusion of two parts of hydrogen with one of oxygen. We will leave on one side the mystery of how an electrical discharge can cause this fusion and ask only whether this scientific definition is a satisfactory account of water. Here I will venture to borrow from John Baillie's Gifford Lectures a quotation from George Macdonald:

What, I ask, is the truth of water? Is it that it is formed of hydrogen and oxygen?... Is it for the sake of the fact that hydrogen and oxygen combined form water, that the precious thing exists? Is oxygen-and-hydrogen the divine idea of water? Or has God put the two together only that man might separate them and find them out?... The water itself, that dances, and sings, and slakes the wonderful thirst—symbol and picture of that draught for which the woman of Samaria made her prayer to Jesus—this lovely thing itself, whose very sweetness is a delight to every inch of the human body in its embrace... this water is itself its own truth, and is therein a truth of God. Let him who would know the love of the maker become sorely athirst, and drink of

the brook by the way—then lift up his heart—
not at that moment to the maker of oxygen and
hydrogen, but to the inventor and mediator of
thirst and water, that man may foresee a little of
what his soul may find in God. . . . As well may
a man think of describing the joy of drinking by
giving thirst and water for its analysis, as imagine
he has revealed anything about water by resolving
it into its scientific elements. Let a man go to the
hillside, and let the brook sing to him till he
knows it, and he will find himself far nearer the
fountain of truth than the triumphal car of the
chemist will ever lead the shouting crew of his
half-comprehending followers. He will draw
from the brook the water of joyous tears 'and
worship him that made heaven, and earth, and
the sea, and the fountains of water'.[1]

This is, of course, a highly rhetorical and poetical
passage; it carries us far beyond anything my previous argument has justified; it is theological.
Moreover, the poet is only describing what water
is, or may be, to *man*. None the less, even the least
poetical or theologically minded reader may agree
that the poet gives us a better account of what water
is in the real world of our experience than any
more exact definition of it in terms of H_2O.

But suppose a scrupulous or prosaic objector says,
'the poet has merely been describing what water
(sometimes) *seems* to be; the scientist by his experiments shows what water really *is;* the poetic fancy
is delightful, but it is far removed from scientific

[1] *Unspoken Sermons*, 3rd series, pp. 67 ff.. quoted in *The Sense
of the Presence of God*, Oxford, 1962, p. 45.

truth'. What should we answer him? We should, I think, give a double answer. First we should remind him that his initial supposition 'there is no truth but scientific truth' is not itself a scientific truth; it is a (very disputable) theory. He starts from a 'truth' which on his own theory cannot be a truth. The delight of swimming is as much a truth about water as that water is composed of oxygen and hydrogen. It is a direct truth of experience as the latter is not. Second, we should point out that the scientists like the rest of us are dealing with phenomena, that is, with the world as it appears to human senses even when the range of these senses is extended by the microscope or other delicate instruments. They may accurately tell us that the phenomenon of water as it appears to man is oxygen and hydrogen in fusion; they may analyze these two elements yet further and further, but in the end how an electrical discharge turns H_2O into water is a mystery, a mystery of units of energy that may be postulated but literally cannot be imagined. Water is part of the physical or material universe. We know well (and George Macdonald has poetically expressed for us) what water means to *man;* what matter is in itself we cannot know. The scientist's assertion that water is two parts hydrogen and one part oxygen is, no doubt, true and interesting, but it is a very small part of the truth about water.

In this chapter, then, I have maintained that things really are but are not what they seem. If we would know what things really are in themselves, we must ask the physicists, and they will give us an answer which we shall accept as provisional, for the mystery of matter ultimately eludes the vision of the physicists and has to be described by them in terms of that which our minds cannot imagine. Things really are, but in the world of our experience of them all the adjectives that we apply to them, hot, cold, hard, soft, blue, green, beautiful or noisome are descriptions of them not as they are in themselves but as they appear to human senses. In some way, then, the mind itself creates the world of our experience. None the less there is a real world which we explore, and our explorations, the deeper they go, tend to be expressed in formulae of mathematics. In so far as this is so, the work of scientists may be described as mind exploring Mind. Further, all scientific investigation rests upon the idea of causation which we express in terms of the 'laws of nature', and all our experience of things is in time and space. For instance, if I am stung by a wasp, I receive a stimulus from my brain and indirectly from the wasp, but when holding up my finger, I say, 'I feel it *here* and I feel it *now*', the 'here' and 'now' are not part of the stimulus; they are forms or conditions under which I can have experience of things. Cause, time and space are mental forms or conditions of human experience; they are contributions of the mind to the experience of things. Finally, using the illustration of water, I indicated that our experience of things far exceeds the bare *data* of the senses. Things are most mysterious.

3

Nature

WE HAVE considered 'things', but modern scientific investigation seems to have removed the rigid and absolute distinction between the organic and the inorganic. We must think of Nature as a *living* whole. Nature is not a static system of mathematical patterns and causal laws; it is a vast process that we have come to call emergent Evolution. Why and how did the original protons and electrons gather themselves into gases and then form solids with all the various metals, and then produce life and the extraordinary proliferations of life in plants and fish and birds, in animals and insects? How and why did they in the end give birth to man? We have to consider life and not merely mathematics.

R. S. Franks put the matter thus:

A great deal that is important slips through the

net of mathematical relations. It may be possible to reduce the universe from a mathematical point of view to electrons, protons and radiation. But we still have to explain why different numerical combinations of electrons and protons should produce the various chemical elements which are so qualitatively diverse; why these elements, again, should combine in various proportions to form compounds qualitatively different from them and from each other; why from these compounds the whole variety of the universe should proceed; why some combinations should form the basis of life, vegetable, animal and human; why human life should develop as it does in all the variety and wonder of the story of man upon the earth; why finally states and civilizations, heroes and prophets, should appear in the history of human progress.[1]

Franks goes on to say that the only apparent explanation of all these things is 'teleological'; that is to say, some purpose is being served. But can we really detect purpose in natural processes, and what do we mean by Nature? 'Evolutionary progress', writes Sir Alister Hardy, 'is now seen to be due as much to the developing psychic life of the species as to the blind action of the environment'.[2]

[1] R. S. Franks, *The Atonement*, pp. 116 f.
[2] *The Divine Flame*, Collins, 1966, p. 34.

I

Recently (1968) there was published a book of unusual interest by a young scientist, a Nobel Prize winner, who tells from a personal point of view the story of his remarkable discovery.[1]

He worked with a small group of fellow-scientists in his race against scientists elsewhere. We read of the surprises and disappointments, the bye-paths and no thoroughfares, the inspirations and dejections which marked his course, as also of the friendships, the rivalries, the animosities, the contempts, the personal strains and personal ambitions which underlay his scientific work. But chiefly we are caught up in the overmastering intellectual excitement of the chase. The author with his colleagues is said to have discovered the structure of DNA, which is short for deoxyribonucleic acid, and this is of high scientific importance because, it would seem, genes are made of DNA, which is therefore the molecule of heredity, and these young scientists claim, it appears, to have 'found the secret of life'.[2] So absorbing was the search at times that the author could 'lose all interest in the outside world'.[3] True, he is at pains to tell us that affairs, or at least titillations, of the heart alleviate the tempestuous effervescence of the intellect, but the impression made by the book as a whole is of the overwhelming and exclusive

[1] J. D. Watson, *The Double Helix*, Weidenfeld and Nicolson, 1968.

[2] *Op. cit.*, p. 197.   [3] *Op. cit.*, p. 77.

devotion of the scientist to the discovery of how Nature works. Nature is there to be unravelled by the prying and devoted intellect of man.

It may well be that the author does not here reveal his deepest thoughts about his research, but in his book, as he has written it, I found no trace of awe or reverence before the beautiful and mysterious workings of Nature here revealed. 'The secret of life' is not laid bare by a discovery of the almost unimaginably complex working of the mechanism of a molecule. Only a very young man could suppose it is. We admire and respect and praise and value the patient and devoted work of scientists, but if their researches leave them and us without a sense of awe and reverence,

> Great God! I'd rather be
> A Pagan suckled in a creed outworn,
> So might I, standing on this pleasant lea,
> Have glimpses that would make me less forlorn;
> Have sight of Proteus rising from the sea,
> Or hear old Triton blow his wreathed horn.

It is not possible for modern man to revert to the old mythologies. If events happened by Chance, or if Proteus rising from the sea or Triton winding his horn could arbitrarily interfere with the order of Nature, there could be no science; the author's scorn of traditional theologizings is understandable enough, but the discoveries of the scientists leave us only forlorn, if there is nothing to be said about the universe beyond a description of how it works. It is very pardonable that in the excitement of the chase the young scientist should overlook both the pre-suppositions and the implications of his own endeavours. The presupposition of the scientist is that he is studying a rational order; mind is exploring Mind. But what are the implications of Nature as a process?

II

It would seem unreasonable to ascribe intelligence or purpose to the original protons and electrons from which, it appears, all the ordered universe proceeds, but, unless we are willing according to traditional theological ideas to ascribe all development to the direct intervention of a Supreme Being, it is necessary to ascribe to the protons and electrons some innate tendency to form themselves into crystals and metals and then into the infinitely various forms of life. The process lasting through untold millenia is *as if* within the protons and electrons, and then within the chemical compounds, there were some kind of groping, a guided groping, whereby, when the appropriate circumstances arrive, each new stage is reached.

We find in Nature that which corresponds to intelligence in man, but in Nature as a whole we detect no clear-cut purpose. We find purposive action here and there, no doubt; the sparrows build their nest and lay their eggs for the purpose, presumably unknown to them, of the preservation of the species, but no human being can guess or imagine what purpose is served by the Milky Way or by those stars which appear and then explode, having, so far as we can see, accomplished nothing. From the fact that we find purpose here and there in Nature, dare we infer that purpose is inherent in the Whole? The animal world, as Lotze says:

> presents in many instances a dazzling appearance of adaptation to ends, but undeniably, at the same time, much that is inexplicable, much that, so far as we can see, is purposeless, myriad oddities of formation that are easily understood as sports and casual effects of a Nature joyously breaking out in all possible directions, but only with laboured artificiality can be construed as products of deliberate design. Still less can the idea of predetermined adaptation be traced through the vegetable kingdom, where no end can be pointed out beyond the mere existence of forms, whose arrangement, duration, development and power of self-preservation present endless differences in kind and amount.[1]

The world appears as 'an impressive stupendous reality'; to what shall we ascribe it but to 'a predominant fate willing nothing but itself'? To science the Whole, whether it be called Nature or Fate, is ultimately meaningless.

Many scientists are of the opinion that there are probably unnumbered planets in the universe capable of sustaining life and therefore possibly inhabited by human beings. Indeed, it is just possible that we are already being visited from worlds beyond.[2] But these speculations are not

[1] *Op. cit.*, I, 420 f.

[2] *vide* J. and J. Vallee, *A Challenge to Science*, with a foreword by Prof. Hynek, Spearman, 1967.

helpful for our present purpose. We know nothing of what life there may be beyond our planet, but about our own planet we know much; we can with much confidence trace its history, and we know what it is today.

Can we find purpose in the story of our earth? We must rule out Chance; we must recognize Contingency. We must rule out Chance because Chance is incompatible with science. If it were just by chance that touching a red-hot poker caused pain, we might properly hope that next time it would not have that effect. Everything has a cause; that is the ground-axiom of science. Nothing occurs by chance. But Contingency (for which we often carelessly use the name chance) is another matter. The contingent is that which might, or might not, occur. I plant an acorn in the garden. Whether or not it will grow into an oak is quite unpredictable; the frosts may get it; it may be choked by the vegetation around it; it may get cut down inadvertently by a scythe or trampled by some dog into the ground; but given the right conditions it is bound to grow into an oak. It has, we might say, an innate purpose to become an oak, though this purpose may be thwarted; there will be a cause for its fate whatever that fate may be; nothing is uncaused. The long story of Evolution is a tale of the unpredictable, but not of the uncaused. For all that we know, life might have appeared millenia earlier or later than was the case on our earth, but when the appropriate chemical and electrical conditions appeared, it was necessary and inevitable that life should issue as the result. No scientist can say more than that, unless some unpredictable contingency (such as a random behaviour of electrons or a cosmic disturbance) should occur, then certainly and necessarily this will follow that.

The sphere of the unpredictable or contingent is vast, but as we look over the course of Evolution, we observe what we must call progress from the undifferentiated to the ever more highly differentiated. It is as if by endless experiments and by an innate and unconscious groping a habitable world came into being, then life arrived and, much later, man with his reason and his power to contemplate the process. It is not by chance but by some innate necessity that the gases produced the solid earth with its various elements, that in due course, when the time was ripe and the required conditions arose, life first appeared, then man with his reason, his strange ideals and his hopes.

The canal which is of man's contrivance runs, so far as possible, in a straight line from point to point; no pleasant wandering over the country-side for the canal! But the river meanders through the fields, twists and winds and not infrequently turns back upon itself till in the end it loses itself in the bosom of the sea. We are apt to think of purpose in terms of the canal:

> *That low man seeks a little thing to do,*
> *Sees it and does it:*

But
> *This high man, with a great thing to pursue,*
> *Dies ere he knows it.*[1]

[1] Browning, *A Grammarian's Funeral.*

A man may set his heart upon improving the housing conditions in his neighbourhood; he may first appeal to the Parish Council with no result; he may turn to the Rural District Council and after much delay find nothing done; he may then appeal to various charities; and his request meet with refusal; he may try to interest the Press, and find there no response; he may before he die have interested a few more affluent neighbours and made a small beginning. His purpose will have been unswerving from first to last, but his course will have been as devious as that of the river. If in outline we can trace a development and progress in the story of our planet from a gaseous mass through the inorganic, as we call it, up to life with its innumerable varieties and then to man, a rational being, and if all this story and intricate, involved development of interdependent elements cannot be ascribed to chance, it looks *as if* within Nature herself there was a purpose gradually being realized in spite of many set-backs and false starts.

When we try to imagine the innumerable human beings who crawl and have crawled over the earth's surface and in the streets and alleys of our cities in hunger, in poverty, in pain and misery, we may be disposed to conclude that the vast parturition of the ages has brought forth a ridiculous and ill-formed mouse; for man, Nature's highest achievement, is the most unhappy and discontented of her creations; but the end of the story is not yet, and we may look further. If in our pessimism we want to say that Nature's purpose was bad or misconceived, the word 'purpose' cannot easily be avoided.

III

I suppose we might say that the molecules behave in a kind of instinctive way, but we reserve the term 'instinct' for the strange and purposive behaviour of the animal world and allow this word to cover and to suffocate our wonder at the marvels of natural history. Who taught the beaver how to build its dam, the bees how to build their hives and organize their lives, the swallows to emigrate across the trackless deep and return to their old nests when the days grow warm enough in the country of their birth? It is certain that no first father beaver ever thought out the construction of the dam, that no primal statesman in the bee family ever planned a hive or decided upon the organization and ranking of the bee society, and the travels of swallows are not consciously planned as we plan our holidays. We offer no explanation, we merely enlarge upon the mystery when we say that Nature implants in animals their instincts.

Many biologists stifle the wonder by employing scientific terms; they speak, not of Nature, but of Mutation and of Natural Selection. This is to shrug off the mystery by saying that in the course of Evolution living creatures are changed and certain forms are chosen for survival. But we must turn these into active verbs and ask, Who changes, who is it that selects? We answer, Nature; and

Coleridge is said to have spoken of the difficulty of deciding whether nature is 'a goddess in petticoats or a devil in a straight-waistcoat'. I will be content with the term 'goddess'.

Here we have all manner of creatures acting with an astonishing intelligence, and it is certain that the intelligence is not their own. The intelligence, we say, is immanent in Nature, but here we have personified Nature as a rational being, a goddess (or a god), and this is the world of mythology and phantasy. Nature will be a goddess like the figures of old Greek mythology which we might fear or respect but certainly could not adore. It would be improper for us to require of the scientists as such to say more than Nature or Mutation or Natural Selection, but as man's study of the mathematical aspects of Nature must be described as mind discovering Mind, so in the sphere of biology mind is discovering Mind. Since the universe is one, and its parts are marvellously balanced and interrelated, the Mind that is being explored is one. We may picture Dame Nature as a goddess, but this is sheer mythology unless that picture correspond to some ultimate Reality which must be conceived as transcendent and as being at least in this limited sense personal that He or She or It must be called Mind. Because the universe is one and not self-explanatory, we are, I judge, really forced by logic to postulate some Reality whose Power or Energy and Intelligence are manifested in natural processes and in Evolution.

It has been traditional in the West to speak, not of Nature, but of God. I prefer here, however, to keep to the term Nature, for 'God' is a word of religion, and religion is not yet in sight. The world that we enjoy and study is a whole, a unity, a rational order. We cannot ascribe its appearances to a number of gods and goddesses, Aphrodite, Dionysus, Apollo, Pan, Diana and the like. The Power and Intelligence that forms the crystals, designs the genes, teaches the plants to grow, the spider to weave the intricacies of its web, the peacock generation after generation faultlessly to produce feathers of the right colour in the appointed order, that constructs the human embryo in the womb we may call Nature spelled with a capital letter. Nature is a mythological term and must represent some Reality, and it is better to say with Lotze that One Being is 'the indispensable presupposition of all intelligibility in finite things'[1] but since we are considering a process informed by intelligence and energy, I would, in avoiding the theological and religious word 'God' here, rather speak of a Presence or a Spirit that must be conceived as in some sense transcendent as well as immanent.

IV

This word 'nature' can bear various meanings which I must here distinguish clearly. Nature, we say, teaches the birds to build their nests, the spider to construct its web. Nature here stands for the mysterious Power and Intelligence which is immanent within the evolutionary order and yet

[1] *Op. cit.*, II. 659.

must be conceived as in some sense transcendent over it, because both the power and the intelligence are imparted to the order. Nature in this sense is presupposed by the scientists and cannot be directly an object of their study. She is Dame Nature or a kind of goddess. Where I so use the term Nature, I spell it always with a capital. In another sense the word nature covers the whole field that is studied in 'the natural sciences'. In this sense nature is directly the object of the enquiries of the scientists, and I spell the word without a capital. There should be no confusion of meaning here. But I cannot wholly escape a third sense of the word, for I cannot avoid speaking of human nature. Man is a child of nature; that is, he arises in the natural order in the course of Evolution; human nature is studied by biologists and psychologists and politicians and sociologists and novelists and dramatists. As an object of scientific study man is a part of nature. On the other hand *we* study nature; here nature is the other than man which he studies; we speak of learning the secrets of nature, using the laws of nature, mastering and taming nature. Here man is extra-natural or supra-natural in his nature. In the previous chapter and in this I have spoken of 'things' which constitute nature and of the mysterious Power and Intelligence informing the whole which I have called 'Nature' with a capital. Now, somewhat anticipating my next chapter I must say a little about human nature.

Here I shall be content to epitomize in a few sentences the idea of human nature as it is expounded with power and at much greater length by

Sir Malcolm Knox in his Gifford Lectures.[1] In the first place, he warns us against 'the genetic fallacy'; we do not discover what science is by contemplating the antics of the witch-doctor; we do not discern the nature of man by contemplating the most primitive forms of man as discovered or supposed by anthropologists or child-psychologists. The germ of human conduct, he tells us, is to be observed in animals; this helps us to understand animals, not men.

Then we must not say that the determinant element in human nature is man's brain or body, because that is a theory, and a theory is a construction of the mind, not of the body. The body is an object; the distinctive element in man is that he is a subject. A little child like an animal acts by instinct, but this is infantile behaviour. Mind is constituted by 'feelings, consciousness, desires, thoughts'. As mind develops, instinct becomes appetite; a baby cries when it is hungry; that is instinct; a child a little older points and says as clearly as if it could speak, 'I am thirsty'; that is appetite. When the child is yet a little older, you may say to it, 'would you like to play a little longer in the garden, or would you like tea now?' In other words we say, 'between various appetites what do you *desire?*' The child has reached the stage of conscious choice; he can begin to act rationally now. At a little higher stage the child can act from a sense of obligation—'I ought to do this, not that'.

[1] *Action*, pp. 30, 38, 44, 45, 47, 52–55, 66–69, 74, 96, 104, 106 f, 164, 191.

In the natural order events occur according to laws which the scientists discover, but man determines himself by a consciousness of law. The determinist or Behaviourist, who holds that all our actions and all our thoughts are biologically determined, represents all our life as a kind of sleep-walking. When I have to decide whether to play golf or go on type-writing, the decision is made by *me*. It is of the essence of human nature that man can choose; he can act rationally; he can, if he will, act conscientiously.

A man can, as we say, 'fail to be himself', but this can never be said of a cat or of a cow. If in a bad moment and contrary to my plain duty I decide to abandon my work for a round of golf, I have failed to be my true self. The moralists say, I have done wrong or evil, but evil is not a positive reality, 'it is a good of too poor a kind'. There have been endless and unfruitful discussions as to whether we have free will, as if the will were some special organ or element in our constitution. Our will is our choice. The question is not whether our will is free, but whether *we* are free. The man who acts under some neurotic compulsion or is at the mercy of some compulsive craving, as for alcohol or heroin, is not free; he cannot choose. We are free only as a rational choice is open to us. To act from rational choice is the meaning and achievement of human nature. We should distinguish action from mere motion; action is my own. Action brings the non-existent into existence, it is 'mind translating itself into actuality'.

I have translated the pages of a master into a few short paragraphs, but have said enough to indicate where human nature is to be distinguished both from Nature and from nature. Man not only knows, as my first chapter indicated; he can also choose; to choose aright or rationally is the meaning or perfection or realization of human nature.

So a philosopher speaks of man. Let us hear also from another aspect a biologist. Sir Alister Hardy, who fully agrees with Dr. Polanyi that 'all human knowledge is now seen to be shaped and sustained by the inarticulate mental faculties which we share with the animals', says this of the appearance of man in the course of Evolution:

The brevity of man's evolution is even more surprising when we contemplate what has happened within this tiny fraction—perhaps no more than a thousandth—of the time living organisms have been upon the earth. We saw how man, by the development of his culture, has altered the very nature of the living stream itself; not only has he dominated the whole of the animal world, but he has changed the method of his own evolution from a largely Darwinian to a largely Lamarchian one. By the development of speech, and with it reasoning powers, man has provided himself with a new form of inheritance; by the spoken, written and printed word, and by all manner of new methods of communication, he can pass on to later generations all the newly acquired knowledge and experience obtained in his lifetime. Life has passed into a new phase; one which differs as fundamentally from that of ordinary animal life as animals differ from plants.[1]

Finally (for man's distinctive nature is not yet fully expressed) we may consider a few lines from Juvenal, the pagan satirist:

Nature, by her own confession,
*   gave the human race soft hearts,*
*   to them only the gift of tears.*
This element of pity
*   is the finest part*
*   of our sensible being. . . .*
It is Nature's imperative we groan and sigh
when a girl dies in the flower of her youth
or a child is buried too young for the funeral pyre.
What man worthy to hold a torch at the Mysteries,
what man worthy to be a celebrant of Ceres
ever considers that another's troubles are not his own?
Is not this what divides us from
'the inferior creatures mute,
irrational and brute?'[2]

V

If I am shown a piece of machinery and given an explanation of how its parts are related to one another and how they work, I assume without being told that the engine is devised to serve some purpose, though I may be utterly unable to guess what that purpose is. The universe, as studied by the scientists, is not strictly a piece of machinery,

[1] *The Divine Flame*, pp. 41, 35.
[2] Satire XV ll. 132 ff. Charles Plumb's translation.

but we inevitably ask the question, 'what is it for? What purpose does it serve?'

If we think of the Milky Way, we have no clue to the answer, and there are those who are content to say that the universe is not 'for' anything, that it serves no imaginable purpose; it is just there, a fact not open to rational explanation. But it is more difficult to take that view when our own planet, of which we know so much more, is under consideration. We can in outline trace its history from its earliest forms to the arrival of rational man, who, as we know him, is the latest but not necessarily the final product of the evolutionary order. It looks as if there must be a purpose in this story. It is not helpful to speak of 'a dreaming soul of the universe', nor sensible to speak of a blind purpose which would be a contradiction in terms. We presuppose and we find reason in the order, but we cannot sensibly suppose that there is reason *in* the order but no reason *for* the order. But if we are seeking the reason *for* the order, we are more likely to see it or to glimpse it by looking at its highest achievements than at its first beginnings. We shall say that the purpose, or at least one purpose, of Nature is to produce man, whatever later developments there may be.

'Is cosmic history', asks Lotze, 'nothing but the infinitely narrow and incessantly changing streak of light which we call *the present*, glimmering between the obscurity of a past which is done with and is no longer anything, and the obscurity of a future which is also nothing?'[1] That way madness

[1] *Op. cit.*, II. 712.

lies or at least total unintelligibility, but it is the mind alone which holds together the past, the present and the future.

Science studies the world of phenomena; we apprehend all phenomena in terms of space and time and cause. These are not real things but modes of our experience. We must postulate as the ultimate ground of phenomena an innumerable number of units of energy that in themselves are neither temporal nor spatial. 'A particle', said Eddington, 'may have position or it may have velocity, but it cannot in any exact sense have both'. 'There *is* nothing else', said Lotze, 'but an eternal inner stream of reciprocal action in things'.[1] We apprehend an (entirely non-theological) 'trinity in the cosmos, laws *according to* which things are, powers *by* which things are, and ends *for the sake of* which they are'.[2]

The tendency and aim of reason is 'to bring the actual world into the unity of an harmonious whole', to find the rationale of its relations and to apprehend them in terms of meaning; but meaning is for mind alone. As we have in these later years come to apprehend Nature as a unity, our thought is in some degree representative of the archetypal Thought, whatever it be, of which Nature is the expression. We can neither dispense with scientific enquiry nor stop short of it, for science itself points to that which is beyond itself.

I would sum up my first three chapters. I have given reasons for supposing that *we* exist; I have asserted

[1] *Op. cit.*, II. 622.   [2] *Id.* II. 487.

65

the genuine existence of 'things' but indicated that we know them only as phenomena, that is, as they appear to human beings, estimating the contribution of mind to our experience of things. Then, having biology more particularly in view, I have considered Nature as a process of things, manifesting reason or intelligence and suffused with the strange mystery of life. The process is not self-explanatory; science can say no more than that Nature does this or that, but I have indicated that Nature so spelled with a capital is really a creature of mythology, and while I have tried to avoid the ambiguous term 'God', I have indicated that to account for the process we must postulate a One or Thought, a Presence or a Spirit, of which the whole process, so little intelligible to us, is the expression. I turn back to man.

4

Man as a Person

I

WE SPEAK of man's five senses, of sight, of touch, of hearing, of taste and of smell. It is through these that we are aware of the outside world of things; through our feelings we are aware of that which is not ourselves. But then we also speak of a sense of shame, a sense of honour, a sense of humour, a sense of style and the like; we also speak of common sense. On what ground could we reasonably claim that our traditional or corporeal five senses put us in touch with reality, but that the senses I have just named are purely subjective and bring no evidence of that which is not ourselves? It is true that a sense of humour or a sense of style has not its own physical organ like an eye or ear, but these non-corporeal senses, as John Baillie said, 'enable us to perceive something not otherwise perceptible'.[1]

[1] *The Sense of the Presence of God*, Oxford, 1962, p. 53.

For instance, P. G. Wodehouse has written many humorous stories; if we have no sense of humour, we shall miss the point and, presumably, be merely bored by them, but we shall have missed something that is there to be recognized; or, to take a much more serious instance, if I were to say, 'I have no sense of the Presence of God', that would, of itself, be no proof that God was not present or that others were not apprehending reality when they alleged this sense. We have corporeal senses whereby we are aware of things, and we have non-corporeal senses, such as a sense of justice or of fair play, whereby we are aware of non-corporeal aspects of the world of our experience. But our corporeal and our non-corporeal senses can play us false, as when we think something square which is really oblong, or think something funny which is really tragic; but it is entirely arbitrary to claim that our corporeal senses give us knowledge of a real world, while our incorporeal senses merely tell us about our own subjective feelings. It is not only through our physical senses that we are aware of the world about us; in other words, science only deals with one aspect of our experience.

'The world as it is', wrote W. R. Inge, 'is not good enough to be true. We ought not to be satisfied with it'.[1] Lotze put it in this way, that 'insight into what ought to be will alone open our eyes to discern what is'.[2] We should never judge a room to be dirty and untidy, if we did not know that it ought to be clean and tidy. We should

[1] *Personal Religion and the Life of Devotion*, Longmans, Green, p. 60. [2] *Op. cit.*, I. 392.

never call a man bad, unless we knew that men should be good. That is, apart from just moral and aesthetic judgements we do not know the truth about the world of our experience. We stand outside or above nature and declare what ought to be but is not. This power of moral and aesthetic judgement is at least as essential as scientific information for understanding the world in which we live.

The other animals take life as it comes; man is the discontented animal, for, however hard he strives, he never quite achieves his ideal, and even his rare moments of ecstasy are marred by transience. Nothing in life gives rise to the *experience* of perfection, but the perfect, the eternal, the infinite are notions which man intuitively understands. Living in a world of imperfection, of transience and finitude he strives after perfection, mourns over transience and struggles against the limitations of his finitude.

Man is moved by ideals, but a transcendent ideal is by definition that which does not exist. Beauty and Truth and Perfection are abstract nouns and being abstractions have no existence of their own. It is therefore not unnaturally claimed that man's ideals are his dreams, and there is no reality corresponding to them. Now, it may always be under the stimulus of some sense impression that we awaken to the demands of ideal beauty or goodness or perfection, but the sense of imperfection giving rise to the ideal in our minds is never itself given in the impress of the senses. Man is drawn, uplifted and inspired by his ideals of beauty, of goodness, of perfection; he does not inspire himself, and the sensible impression itself cannot inspire him. But that which does not exist cannot act. There must be *Something* therefore which quickens his imagination and inspires his life. 'Man knows his finitude and imperfection', says Sir Malcolm Knox, 'only because the infinite and its perfection somehow dwells within him as spirit warring against nature', and, again, 'morality consists in moulding the finite in accordance with the claims of the infinite'.[1] Truth, Goodness, Beauty, Perfection may be abstract nouns but they represent an active Agency.

There is an old Greek saying, going back to Aristotle, that 'Nature does nought in vain'. Natural Selection, as we call it, leads the plant, the insect, the fish, the animal, the bird to adapt itself ever better to the environment in which it finds itself. The highest form of life which Nature so far has produced is man who is for the first time aware of an environment of the ideal which presses upon his spirit. It would be in the highest degree anomalous if man's ideals, which are the noblest, the highest, the most distinctive element in his nature, correspond to no reality at all; it would be as if birds had developed wings with no sky in which to fly. It would be natural to suppose that some infinite Spirit were impinging upon the human spirit, and we may well ask whether the call of beauty, of obligation and of perfection is not merely demand but also promise or foretokening.[2] The finite, says Sir Malcolm Knox, 'implies its opposite; to describe something as finite is to

[1] *Action*, pp. 107, 222.

[2] *v.* Peter Baelz, *Theology and Metaphysics*, p. 67.

presuppose an infinite, and it is against the background of the infinite alone that the finite is intelligible'.[1]

II

All the adjectives we ascribe to things or events, such as hard, soft, beautiful, ugly, sweet, bitter, heroic, dastardly are expressions of the values we as human beings ascribe to them. We clothe the world of forms or events with the cloak of human values, practical, moral or aesthetic. There is no thinking apart from feeling, no feeling apart from valuation, and every adjective expresses value.

Because of the necessary unlikeliness of men to one another there are many who would make a distinction in respect of values. Some, they would say, are universally valid, for we all agree about the solidity of a cricket-ball; other values, such as the alleged beauty of a Titian or a Bach Cantata are private, particular, personal; for some men have no eye or ear for beauty, and men differ as widely in their aesthetic as in their moral judgements. Some take pleasure in art and music, it is said, and some do not spare a thought to them; it is all a matter of taste, and truth does not come into the question at all; there is no truth but the valid truths of science which are true for all men equally.

Now, some people like liquorice sticks, and others, of whom I am one, do not. This is a matter of taste about which quarrelling would be silly.

[1] *Action*, p. 30.

The disagreement may be due to childhood experiences or to chemical differences in the body. But if I say that Shelley's Ode to Mont Blanc is beautiful, I conceive myself to be asserting as universal or valid or certain a truth about the Ode as if I said that my copy is printed in black ink. I should not read the Ode to little children and expect them to think it beautiful, and there are many adults who would be as unimpressed as children; but when I say that Ode is beautiful, I am not merely saying that the reading of it gives me pleasure (for why should anyone be interested in my likes and my dislikes?), rather I am calling on my hearer to read the Ode, if he has not done so, being certain that, if he be an educated man, he will be moved by it as I am. I am telling him something about the Ode, not about myself. Or if I should say, 'Mozart's *Cosi fan Tutte* is to me just a succession of sounds; I would as soon listen to the orchestra tuning up', I should have expressed as false and foolish a judgement as if I had said that a cricket ball is square; I have failed to apprehend that which was there to be apprehended. Judgements or valuations in art can be true or false as judgements in chemistry or physics.

We should do well to consult the artists about this. It is true that I derive pleasure from reading the *Faerie Queene* or *Paradise Lost* or *The Testament of Beauty*, but it is quite certain that Spenser and Milton and Bridges did not regard their work in the light of popular entertainment. They did not toil and labour in order to titilate pleasurable sensations in the reader. We are familiar with stories of artists who live in garrets and on starvation diet because, being dedicated to the pursuit of beauty, they will not condescend to be purveyors of mere pleasure. Again, we make a distinction between the pretty and the beautiful; both, it may be said, give pleasure, but beauty gives a higher kind of pleasure; but here we have introduced a new element into the situation if we require a scale of pleasure. That which is pretty catches our fancy; that which is beautiful evokes a different response. The picture on a glossy magazine may be pretty and evoke a momentary sense of pleasure; a portrait by Rembrandt is not pretty at all; it is beautiful; it evokes not happiness, I should say, but joy. The artists, the poets, the musicians, whose labours of composition are so arduous and sometimes agonizing are seeking, not to entertain us, but to shew us what they have seen and felt; it is a truth they are trying to express, though in the case of the painter and the musician it be a truth which cannot be set in words. 'To me', wrote Wordsworth,

> the meanest flower that blows can give
> Thoughts that do often lie too deep for tears.

It is those *thoughts* which in his poetry Wordsworth seeks to express. Every form of artistic expression is an attempt to set forth the *truth* as the artist sees it, though in the case of lesser artists it may be only some miserable little truth about themselves.

III

It would be very natural for anyone with an ear for music to say, 'Beethoven speaks to me'. It would be unkind and foolish to reply 'well, what does he tell you?', for that which his music conveys is, indeed, apprehended by the mind but is not to be set down in words or sentences. I should say that Beethoven speaks to me, though I, who have small knowledge and understanding of music, may wholly misinterpret or fail to grasp that vision with which Beethoven was agonizing when he wrote down those tremendous chords. There is no doubt, however, that his music, however poorly understood, is some sort of personal communication from the musician to the listener. So with great painting or great poetry the beginner may grasp but little, or may even misinterpret, what the painter or the poet would convey to him, but he receives some message, not, it is likely, in the form of anything that could be put into a sentence and parsed and analyzed, but in the form of an illumination of the mind, a quickening of the heart, an elevation of the spirit. This message is not to be defined. 'Intuition is our thinking become luminous'.[1]

Everyone knows how impossible it would be to answer the question, 'what do you get from listening to Beethoven or going round the Uffizzi gallery?' To reply that you get pleasure might, no

[1] Knox, *Action*, p. 139.

doubt, be true, but it would be a shrugging off of the question; your whole person has been shaken; your mind or soul or heart or whatever you like to call the core of your personality has been moved through the feelings imparted to you. You are, or you feel called to be, a better or a wiser man. You have received, however far you have failed to grasp, a personal communication from the artists. Flickering mind has been in contact with greater minds.

It seems to me a matter of sheer prejudice and quite irrational when any man says, 'I agree that from the artist, the musician, the poet in the beauty he has produced I received some personal communication' and then denies this of the wonder, the delight, the awe with which he regards the beauty of nature. When we contemplate the universe with its mathematical patterns, its intricate order and its mutual adaptation of parts, we are constrained to postulate that which for scientific purposes may be called Nature spelled with a capital, but which from the philosophical point of view is the One that stands behind the whole, or the Mind or Thought which the human mind is able in some small degree to find and recognize in Nature. The voice, so to call it, which speaks to us through great mountain scenery or the sight of a cornfield swept by the wind or the rippling of the brook through the trees and meadows is the voice of Nature; then it is the voice, or a voice, of the One, the Mind or Thought of which the natural order is the articulate expression. As in the mathematical aspects of

Nature, so in natural beauty mind is in contact with Mind, or, if we prefer to use more poetical language, heart with Heart.

IV

As a table is a solid object, not in itself, but to human sensibility, so an object is not beautiful in itself but only to the eye that so apprehends it. We see beauty in the rainbow that spans the sky on a stormy day, but the beauty is not in the physical object, the bow, for, as we all know, the bow exists only in the eye of man; it is not, where we see it, in the sky. Beauty, we are told, is in the eye of the beholder, and in truth there is no beauty apart from a beholder, but the beholder does not create the beauty that he sees in nature, as he does not create the beauty in a line of Shakespeare; he finds it there. It comes, if at all, as a personal communication; it is transmitted to him *through* but not *in*, the material and physical.

There is an intimate connection between truth and beauty. If a man should look at the snows and cataracts and bastions and peaks of Mont Blanc and say, 'yes, very pretty', we should call him Philistine; we who are quite incapable of writing Coleridge's *Hymn Before Sunrise in the Vale of Chamouni* look upon Mont Blanc as he did with wonder and with awe. Now, wonder and awe may perhaps be called pleasurable sensations; pleasure is perhaps their concomitant but it is not their essence:

Thou hast a Voice, great Mountain, to repeal
Large codes of fraud and woe; not understood
By all, but which the wise, and great, and good
Interpret, or make felt, or deeply feel.

Was Shelley wrong, and not merely incorrect, in saying that Mont Blanc had a voice? He and Coleridge did their best to put into words what that great Voice said to them. We according to our sensitivity can enter into their experience. The great mountain speaks to all of us; what it says, is not something about the mountain itself but something deeper—about life or reality or existence. When we call the mountain beautiful or awe-inspiring, we are not really calling attention to our feelings, we are saying that it speaks to us, that it does something to us, it causes us to see more than eye can see, it speaks in a language for which any words of ours must be inadequate, and we are summoning others to this experience of *reality*.

There is this difference between the hardness of a cricket ball and the beauty of Mont Blanc in that the hardness of the one is a common, universal experience subject to scientific definition, the beauty of the other is appreciable according to the development of our sensibilities. But on what grounds should we be justified in saying that one judgement was objective and real, and the other subjective and imaginary? It is through the eye that we see Mont Blanc from the Vale of Chamouni, but what the mountain says to us is not a matter of our physical senses at all. Physical objects like mountains and cricket balls are real in that they belong to the world of sensible experience, but what they ultimately *are*, even the physicists do not avail to tell us; they have a subjective reality only. But what the mountain says to us is direct, objective and immediate, however imperfectly we hear what it has to say. It speaks of that which is beyond or outside the world of sense.

Since we are impressed by the impact of its physical characteristics upon our 5 corporeal senses!

V

Nothing in this world is perfect, nothing is unchanging, all is relative, it can be measured and has its price upon the market; but upon beauty it is not possible to put a price. True, we can sell an Old Master at Sotheby's for a nameable figure, but that beauty and perfection after which the artist strives, the beauty that 'catches us by the throat', is of unconditional or infinite or absolute and measureless worth. The pursuit and recognition of beauty is a kind of instinct in man, though instinct is not technically the proper term. The wonder, the awe, the reverence evoked by Beauty is a very mysterious element in human nature, deserving close attention when we raise the question whether human life has any meaning; for here and there human life is touched and illuminated by a sense of the timeless, the unconditioned, the absolute or infinite.

I have dwelt upon the beauty revealed through Nature as a touch of the timeless, the unconditioned upon the soul or attentive mind of man. It comes to me, however, that of possible readers of these pages most will be town-dwellers who from time to time may get to concerts or picture galleries, but who apart from holidays and occasional strolls in the park will be little in touch with Nature; they will not be able to mark the changes of the sunset, watch the snowdrops come out in the spring-time, smell the scent of new-mown hay or contemplate the changing of the autumnal colours. I would therefore make the same point about human nature from the more familiar aspect of human affection.

I would avoid the word 'love' if I could, for it is put to so many uses. Some love is, I suppose, better called lust and is of the flesh fleshly and no more. But I fancy that all those who have genuinely 'fallen in love' have in their idealizing of the beloved some glimpse of the immeasurable and of a worth beyond all worth, nor would I wish to deny that the lover's ideal picture of the beloved may be a truer vision of the real person loved than the very sober and discriminating judgement of the later obituary columns in *The Times*. But I have chiefly in mind two calmer, deeper forms of love. There is first the love of parents for their children. It is immeasurable, for who would claim to measure it? It is infinite, for literally it knows no bounds. I have in mind, second, the love of husbands and wives when they have lived many long years together, have shared many great joys and many grievous sorrows, and for whom the flames of love leapt high in their youth but are now a deep and abiding and imperishable glow. No human measurement and no imagination can reckon such mutual love; it is boundless, immeasurable, infinite, unchanging, perfect. Here again in the midst of this world of the relative, the impermanent, the imperfect and transient the spirit of man touches, or is touched by, the absolute, the unconditioned, the timeless and the perfect. When we say that 'love is stronger than death', we are asserting that, though the love of parents for their children and the mutual love of husbands and of wives arises out of nature, it transcends and defeats nature; it is, as it were, the triumph of the eternal over the transient, the infinite grasped for a moment by the finite. The object of love is not an idea or an ideal, but a reality. Its source is not in nature but beyond this transitory world.

In beauty and in love, in the love of beauty and the beauty of love man is touched by the infinite, the absolute, the timeless and unconditioned. This is a most significant fact about human nature.

VI

Equally mysterious with our sense of Beauty and equally a gift of Nature is man's sense of moral obligation. Men differ in their sense of right and wrong quite as widely as in their aesthetic judgements, but we all recognize a distinction between right and wrong, and all agree that it is right to do right—whatever the right may be, and however difficult it be for us to determine what in the given circumstances is right. It is not granted us to enter into the minds or psychological processes of our most primitive ancestors before the dawn of history, but there can be no question that man in the course of evolution and increasingly as he becomes more and more civilized has an innate sense of duty. He no doubt generally regards it as his duty to follow the rules and conventions of the society in which he finds himself, but duty is not to be identified with conventional conduct. For in the first place moral advance has come as men under an imperative sense of duty have broken with some convention of their age, and in the second the sense of duty is often a very private matter unrelated to convention. When a girl tries to decide whether she should marry the man she loves or stay at home to look after her invalid mother, she is not considering conventions but her duty.

This sense of duty is mysterious. It is a sense of absolute or unqualified obligation. Man touches again, or is touched by, the infinite and unconditioned. It may be his duty to compromise, but it can never be his duty to compromise with his conscience which is the name we give to his sense of duty. Nothing in this world of transience is ever perfect, nothing is good or beautiful without qualification; but because moral obligation, as we recognize, is absolute, unconditional and unqualified, it does not belong to the transient world of nature. Whatever the consequences and at whatever cost we know that we must do our duty. When I say that we *must* do our duty, I do not mean that we are compelled to do it, for indeed we are not. So far as nature is concerned, we are free to neglect our duty but only at the cost of personal integrity. The sense of *must* comes to us not from nature but from beyond. It is rather a denial than an affirmation of nature. Through the natural order we become aware of obligations that transcend that order.

This sense of absolute or unconditional obligation, the binding commandments of duty can never be derived from sensation. It is true that there must be some outward event which evokes in us a sense of obligation, but the felt obligation is a contribution of the mind or character to the data of the senses. The awareness of obligation does not come to us from the world of sense. It is both the mark of the nobility and dignity of man and at the same time like a Voice from the Beyond. We have outsights whereby through our senses we are aware of the world about us, but, most clearly in respect of duty, we have insights which are not to be derived from the world of sense.

VII

I have pointed to beauty, goodness and truth as abstract nouns which yet hint at an ultimate Reality, which we may call God. It may be answered that ugliness, wickedness and falsehood are similar abstract nouns. Why should they not point to some ultimate Reality which we may call the Devil? Is not wickedness quite as real as goodness? If we have to believe in God and the devil, we are not only far away from any scientific view of the world but also from any rational explanation of it. But ugliness, wickedness and falsehood are negatives or rather privatives, not positives. If I commission an artist to paint a portrait of the Prime Minister, I may judge his effort to be very bad, ugly and false, but it is a bad, ugly, false portrait only because there is some good in it; if there were no good in it, it would not be a portrait at all. Everything is good in so far as it is what it ought to be; the badness in a portrait or a man or a cricket bat or a musical composition is a failure to achieve the intention of its maker. Evil is a deprivation.

It may be objected that hooliganism and drug-taking and prostitution are positive enough and actual, as indeed they are, and it would seem a monstrous perversion of fact to say that there is good in them. But let us look more closely. Young hooligans are boys with high spirits who seek to find expression for their energies; that is right and good, but too low a good. No one, I suppose, takes drugs for the sake of taking drugs but rather to achieve some good, to find a means of facing life or relieving strain and attain serenity. Prostitution is on the one side a means of attaining pleasure, which is a good, and on the other of earning enough to eat which is also good. If the portrait were not up to a point a good portrait, it would not be a portrait at all. Bad painting or such wickedness as I have named is always a failure to achieve a good.

Sir Malcolm Knox writes:
nothing is wholly and irremediably evil; evil is a negation; the only positive thing in what we reject and call evil is a low degree of goodness.

The law-breaker is wrong and may be called evil, but he may be enjoying himself or achieving his own interest by feathering his own nest, and these are goods. His evil consists in what is *not* there; what *is* there is good, but a good chosen when a higher or more rational choice should have been made, and therefore too low a good in this situation. His evil consists in what he has *not* done.[1]

St. Thomas Aquinas argued that 'if evil is, then God must be' on the ground that only in an order that is intrinsically good can there be evil. Ugliness, moral evil and falsehood are, indeed, abstract terms like beauty, goodness and truth, but they point, not to some ultimate Reality, but to an absence of that which ought to be.

I would sum up the burden of this chapter thus: by means of his five corporeal senses man is aware of his physical environment, but it is through non-corporeal senses (if they may be called senses) that man views his physical environment with wonder, with amusement, with awe or with compassion. A man who lacks a sense of humour or a capacity for reverence is handicapped like a man who is deaf or blind. It would be natural to say, then, that through his physical senses man is aware of a physical environment and through his non-physical senses is aware of a non-physical or 'spiritual' environment. As man on earth is a psycho-physical or body-mind organism, so he is aware of a psycho-physical environment, an

[1] *Action*, p. 186.

environment, that is, which is partly apprehended by his physical senses and partly by his psychic or mental or (in this sense) spiritual senses. The two fields of his experience, the physical and the spiritual, are one single world, for his spiritual experience of humour, of awe, of love, of reverence, of beauty or of a sense of obligation are conveyed to him, or stimulated in him, through the physical. And all the adjectives he uses to describe his experiences—hot or cold, comic or tragic, sublime or ridiculous—are alike his valuations of his experience.

I have urged throughout the chapter that we have no grounds for supposing that, while our physical valuations may be universal and valid and true, our spiritual valuations are wholly unreliable, purely personal and point to no ultimate truth. I urge, finally, that if there be a right response to the physical aspect of our environment, there can be a right response to its non-physical aspect also. Thus, there is a right and a wrong answer to a sum in addition or subtraction; I can estimate rightly or wrongly the distance between A. and B. I may find or miss truth in matters of this kind. I can hear a symphony of Beethoven and make a wrong response in that I have missed the truth he is seeking to convey as only music can convey it. If I see a child fall into the canal, I can make a right or wrong response to that situation. It is as much a *fact* that I ought to go to the child's assistance as it is a *fact* that the child has fallen in.

There is, if only we could find it, a right response to the One, the Thought, the Great Spirit of which we are aware through beauty, through love, through our sense of loyalty, through the demands of a felt obligation. Man's right response to his non-physical environment would be true religion, for these abstract terms, Truth, Goodness, Beauty and the like must point to some Reality of which they are facets or expressions.

'Thou hast a Voice, great Mountain', said Shelley of Mont Blanc. 'Stern Daughter of the Voice of God!', said Wordsworth in his *Ode to Duty*. There must be very few who have no sense of vocation— to be a good housewife, a good mother, a good clerk, to produce a great picture, to write a novel or an ode, to advance the cause of knowledge or to serve humanity. The word 'vocation' comes to us from the Latin for a voice. Our words Truth, Goodness, Justice, Beauty, Perfection are, indeed, abstract nouns, but they represent, or point to, a mysterious Agency or spiritual Activity which is not ours but which calls to us and quickens us.

God is really the only word we have to indicate the One, the Thought or Cause behind all causes and the Reality or Agency which evokes in us a sense of the perfect and bids us give our life for our ideals. This is not to call God *a* Person, for that would be to make God in the image of man; none the less, the Reality which we apprehend with our minds and after which we strive in the pursuit of our ideals must be conceived as personal, not impersonal, for mathematics and truth and goodness and beauty are of the mind and not of things.

I come to the paradoxical conclusion that the scientist who is logical and follows the implications of his work must believe that God is, though he may have no religion, and the artist who gives himself to the pursuit of beauty or the lover of his kind who lives for the service of others loves God, though he never thinks of God. It is said of philosophy, wrote Lotze, 'that if the cup is merely tasted, it leads man away from God, but that if it is deeply drained, it brings him back again'.[1]

[1] *Op. cit.*, II. 446.

Epilogue

THAT IS really the end of my book, but I cannot be wholly content to leave the matter there. I have been writing for persons of intellectual integrity who are puzzled and disheartened by the intellectual temper of the day. I have tried to show that the world in which we live is more mysterious, and that our deeper insights are more trustworthy, than shallow current philosophies allow.

'Lockhart', said the dying Sir Walter Scott, 'I may have but a few minutes to speak to you. My dear, be a good man; be virtuous; be religious; be a good man; nothing else will give you any comfort when you come to lie here'. I am not writing from my death-bed, and it is not permissible for me to take Sir Walter's words upon my lips, but I have been dealing with some of the great issues of human life and destiny, and it may surely be permitted one who has reached the ninth decade of his life to express such personal conclusions as his dim vision will allow.

Whether we are considering chemistry and

physics or biology, the work of the scientists is the story of mind discovering Mind. Discovery is the obverse of revelation. The scientist may say, 'at last I found the right equation', or may equally well say, 'at last the right equation dawned on me'; he might even use a more violent word and say 'the right equation hit me'. The physicists are now reducing matter, once regarded as so indivisible and solid, to units of energy. The whole vast process of Evolution, as we study it, is an expression of some immanent and enormous Energy. Indeed, our own scientific activity is a mode of the Energy that informs the Whole. While, therefore, the scientist may rightly speak of his discoveries, in the last resort the initiative must lie with the transcendent Energy. From another aspect this Energy which is expressed in the mathematical patterns of natural 'laws' and in the most mysterious intelligence shown in animal instinct, is to be conceived as Mind. The ultimate One therefore behind the whole phantasmagoria of existence must be conceived in personal or quasi-personal terms, as He or She rather than as It. But the quality or character of the One cannot be legitimately inferred from any scientific enquiry into the 'laws' of Nature. We may say that God is, but, so far as science is concerned, he is the necessary postulate of thought, the Ineffable, the Inconceivable, the great Unknown.

From the consideration of science I turned to the contemplation of aesthetics and of ethics. Charles Williams has called attention to a remarkable passage in Christopher Marlowe's *Tamberlaine*.

'The beauty of Zenocrate', he says, 'arouses in him (Tamberlaine) something which no hostile army had ever stirred, a sense of defeat, a "conceit of foil". It is a physical sensation of extreme force; kings have not troubled him "so much, by much".' So, Williams concludes, 'Beauty inflicts on man everlasting defeat because in the end man cannot discover and express it in poetry, and therefore not at all. The mind of man discovers that it is not equivalent to the nature of Beauty'.[1] So Wordsworth in *The Prelude* tells us of an overwhelming experience that came upon him:

> *bond unknown to me*
> *Was given, that I should be, else sinning greatly,*
> *A dedicated Spirit.*

In the slangy speech of everyday life Beauty 'hits us in the eye'; we do not create it; it finds us. The initiative comes from without, from the Energy, the Intelligence, the One for whom our name is God.

If Beauty is always a personal word from the artist to the viewer or the hearer, a word not to be expressed in sentences but known only in the response of the heart and mind, so it must be in respect of the beauty that we apprehend in Nature. Why should we mar the gift by failure to recognize and thank the Giver? Why dehumanize ourselves by denying that in some strange way we have been touched by the hand of God?

Ethics may be a subject of surpassing dullness. There is little of inspiration in the thought that we

[1] *Reason and Beauty in the Poetic Mind*, Oxford, pp. 32 f.

must do our duty: we must get up when we had rather remain in bed; we must deal with our correspondence or wash up the breakfast cups and plates; we must go through the routine prescribed by our daily calling and our engagment book. It is, however, very mysterious that unlike the animals we cannot simply take life as it comes; we must deal with it and do our duty. We tell children that they must be good, and we try to be good ourselves; and every now and then we have to make some irrevocable decision:

> *Once to every man and nation*
> *Comes the moment to decide,*
> *In the strife of truth with falsehood,*
> *For the good or evil side.*

To use this word 'nature' in my three senses, we are naturally lazy and naturally selfish and naturally disposed to take the easy path; we have to do battle with nature that we may achieve the dignity of true human Nature. We have a sense of obligation, unqualified and imperative, which comes to us from beyond this world of the relative, the transient, the imperfect.

Moral goodness takes many forms but it is always an expression of good will. This applies to our humdrum duties to our neighbours or our families; it applies to the magnificences of courage that win the Victoria Cross or the George Medal; it applies to gentleness, to chivalry and to the forgiveness of injuries. It is the denial of nature and the assertion of man's super-nature. That we should show good will towards our neighbours comes to us as the imperious voice of duty which we neglect at peril of our true manhood. But this duty of good will cannot be learnt from nature. When Jesus of Nazareth, who was good will incarnate, says 'bless them that curse you; do good to them that despitefully use you; love your enemies', I think that our heart says, Yes. It is no question of accepting traditional standards or conforming to custom; it comes to us as an imperious Voice from the Beyond. As in the case of beauty we apprehend through nature a Voice from the Beyond, from the Energy, the Intelligence, the One that we call God. Goodness in the form of the demands of good will like Beauty *points to* the Beyond.

We could intelligibly say that in the last resort the Truth is God, but we cannot say that God is beautiful, for beauty is a matter of line, of colour, of pattern, of composition or of cadence; nor in any sense of human morality could we say that God is morally good. The Greeks said that the three great virtues are Prudence, Moderation or self-restraint and Courage; all these are obviously inapplicable to God. All that we may claim, and must claim, is that through the demands of moral obligation as through the voice of Beauty we in this world of change and of becoming are in touch with That Which *is*.

It is, indeed, inevitable that we who are so touched should ascribe good will to God.[1] Then we must accept the consequences that follow. If the Beyond is to be conceived as the Source of all

[1] I have preferred the philosophical term 'good will' to the more emotional word 'love', but good will *is* love.

Truth, all Beauty and all Goodness, and if we accept the life of Jesus of Nazareth as the highest example of a life of compassion, unselfishness and forgiveness, then as Professor H. H. Price puts it:[1]

theism of this type is committed to maintaining that God loves sinners as much as saints, fools as much as wise men. More important still, we have to say that he loves those who do not love him as much as those who do. He loves atheists, agnostics and materialists as much as he loves theists—as much, in the sense that his love for each of us is without limit. His love is not only universal, but unconditional. He loves all the persons he has created, whatever they may do, whatever emotional attitudes they may have, whatever their beliefs may be; or rather he loves each of them individually, each for his own sake, as an end in himself. He is indeed *Deus Optimus Maximus*, best as well as greatest. For what could conceivably be better than universal and unconditional love?

But is it true? This, at last, is the question of religion. Our religion is our response to our supersensible experience, to the spiritual world that impinges upon our consciousness through the things of sense. Every man is in some degree aware of God, though he may not give the name of God to that of which he is aware. An artist or a literary man may prostitute his gifts; any man may say No to the call of duty; we can be irreligious only

[1] *Religious Experience and its problems* in *Faith and the Philosophers*, ed. J. Hick.

because we cannot escape the call of the Beyond. I think, however, that most men reading my conclusion will say, 'I wish that this were true; I only wish I could believe it!' There are some who have been brought up to believe this and have never doubted it; they may be counted fortunate. Others by some sudden or gradual *bouleversement* of their spirit are converted to this view and then abide in it; but that experience also has been for the few. To others who would fain believe it but cannot, what can an old man say but, Try it!

There can be no true religion that does not rest upon intellectual integrity; we have no business to make ourselves believe what we do not believe, nor to have our religious faith in one compartment and our daily life and thinking in another. But if you think that my argument may be sound and is certainly not irrational, then try it out. A theory is no use unless it works in practice. You cannot test my conclusion unless you try it out in life.

When a young lad is sent from home to a boarding school, he enters a new world; he adapts himself to it; he has to accommodate himself in new ways to his fellows, to his meals, to his seniors; in a short time if he is adaptable he finds himself at home in his new environment. When he comes home for the holidays, a change is noticed in him—it may be for the better or for worse according to the school, but he is in either case a subtly different person. As we grow up, we all have to adapt ourselves to new circumstances, a change of locality, marriage, new kind of work under new conditions. This we may do voluntarily or of necessity.

Again (but here I write without personal experience) an actor who is to play Hamlet or Macbeth or Lear must feel himself into the part, must, so far as possible, for the time *be* Hamlet or Macbeth or Lear. Then he returns to 'the real world'. What I suggest with much earnestness is that you should determine, let us say for a month or even a week, so far as possible, to live *as if* what Jesus said about his heavenly Father, and *as if* the life he lived of compassion and forgiveness were true. There would be no intellectual lack of integrity in this; you would be in a sense like a scientist trying out some new hypothesis and prepared to abandon it if it did not work, but it must be tried. I think that if you tried so to live for a month or even a week, meditating upon the Ultimate as Jesus conceived him and treating those whom you met as Jesus would see them and treat them, you might come to the conclusion that *this* is real life and all other ways are a delusion. I cannot believe that any man who has ever tried to see his fellows with the eyes of Jesus would ever want thereafter to see them with any other eyes; and if he tried to think of God as Jesus saw him, he might find a fulfilment of the old words, 'and it shall come to pass that before they call I will answer, and while they are yet speaking I will hear'.